The Myth of the Fear of Rejection

Mike Jackson

TABLE OF CONTENTS

ONE

THOSE FEW WORDS

The subject of closing…or, should I say, *not closing*… is clearly a vital subject which is on the mind of every individual on Earth who manages Sales Professionals. Sales Trainers, Sales Coaches, and anyone responsible for the performance of a Sales Team, understand that their Sales Professional's desire and ability to close the deal is paramount to the health and prosperity of the company.

It might be the greatest widget ever conceived, and miracles might have manifested for its manufacture and distribution, but if it is not sold, the company fails. Many companies have manufactured great products and offered the greatest of services - but were forced to close their doors forever due to the lack of Sales.

With the severe consequences of not closing deals in mind, it makes sense that no Sales Professional in their right mind would want to admit to their boss that they were not closing like they should. After all, they would be admitting that at the end of their presentation they just don't say…those few words to close the deal.

However, there are countless Sales Professionals who have acknowledged – when their bosses weren't listening – that they need help closing; they need help with those few words.

Those Sales Professionals inspired me to write this book.

It takes great courage and strong character for any Sales Professional to confess that their presentation is not the greatest, especially any Sales Professional who has achieved some success in their career. A Sales Professional's affirmation that they are not closing like they should would be similar to a professional race car driver admitting that he has a depth perception problem. Respectively, both professionals' bosses would be concerned about their future revenue potential.

Unlike the physical demands of the race car driver, becoming a great closer requires no physical superiority. The *physical* segment of the closing contest is elementary; it requires talking. The real challenge is the *mental* part.

Individuals who are not in Sales, and are not faced with tearing down the mental wall that blocks a person from closing, have little to no insight on how great that challenge is. From the outside looking in, someone not in Sales thinks a 5 year-old could ask, "Do you want to buy it?"

Believe me - it takes one to know one. I sold big-tickets for over 20 years, and I lived through the mental obstacles of closing.

Clearly, by now, you know the words to close with. But in order to be a great closer, you must understand what influences your decision to close - *or not to*. Insight into tearing down that wall blocking you from closing is revealed later in this book. But first, I need to raise your level of awareness about something.

A common denominator with nearly all Sales Professionals is that shortly after they generate just a few Sales, their ego begins to bully their intellect. Often, the Sales Professional falls into the trap of operating in a world of 'knowing it all'. You can't tell them anything about their Sales Presentation because - *they know*. After just a short run of success, the ego influences their thoughts, and the Sales Professional now considers themselves "the best", and the Sales Professional thinks that *they* should have the trainer job.

The Sales Professionals that I have seen achieve the greatest success are Sales Professionals that approach training material with an open mind. They reflect on their strengths and not only identify areas they want to improve, but they also possess a strong desire to take action and improve in those areas.

As I travel the world, it is the same top two areas that I hear Sales Professionals say they want to improve on. Predictably, their Sales Managers agree. The top 2 areas are:

1. Handling areas of concern – A.K.A. objections

2. Closing

Of all of the selling strategies that comprise a company's expectations of what a 'good' Sales Presentation is, closing, or *not closing*, is the most sensitive subject.

In reality, closing is a subject that should be viewed as simply part of the Sales process and not considered differently from any other part. The greeting, qualifying, demonstration, and closing should all be viewed as connected and equal parts of the Sales Presentation. But the majority of Sales Professionals do not view closing as an equal part of the Sales process.

Many Sales Professionals classify closing as a separate subject. To them, closing stands alone, like a single soldier facing an entire enemy battalion. The task of closing is believed by some to be a monumental feat, like climbing Mt. Everest. To them, when it comes time to perform the perceived, arduous task of closing - the oxygen needs to be handy.

Since the 1970s, when I started selling big-tickets, little insight has been shared about the *mental concept* of closing. There are numerous books on "what to say" when you close; yet, ironically, there are only a few different words that across the board will close *any* Sales Presentation.

But the mass majority of Sales Professionals don't say those few words – they just don't close.

Why?

Clearly, one of the biggest pains of Sales Managers on planet Earth is answering the question, "Why don't Sales People close?" Sales Managers bring in top trainers to conduct Sales Training Seminars and hold countless Sales Meetings on the subject of closing; all in an effort to get their Sales Professionals to say those few words… to close!

Good Sales Professionals often make good presentations and get *one sentence* from closing – and then they just don't do it.

Why?

The following pages reveal the answer and will make a profound difference in your selling career.

This is not a "101 Closes to Say" book. Instead, this book is for the Sales Professional that already knows how to ask the simple question, "Do you want to buy it?" or some other small sentence that performs the task of closing. You already know "how to ask" for the sale; you know the words; that's not the focus of this book. The focus of this book is that you just don't close like you should – and you want to get to where you do.

This book will get you there.

In the course of my research for this book, I traveled extensively, sometimes 3 and 4 weeks out of the month, evaluating Sales Professionals as they performed their presentations. After watching thousands of Sales Professionals "work me", and after watching them perform their Sales Presentations all the way down to the point of where they should close, I gained invaluable insight into their thought processes as to why they closed – *or didn't.*

Particular thought processes were repeatedly documented. Although there were times that required attentive evaluation to ascertain exactly why the Sales Professional did not close, the majority of the time the reason was crystal clear.

Previous to launching my Performance Development Company, Progressive Insights, Inc., I successfully sold big tickets for over 20 years. I was privileged to have sold for companies that believed in Sales Training. I learned effective selling strategies and embraced Sales techniques from the finest trainers in the world.

In the course of climbing the ladder of success in my Sales career, I became a professional student. I kept an open mind and absorbed everything the top trainers offered. I took bits and pieces from all of them and applied what worked best for me. It was interesting to see how some selling strategies did not fit me, yet proved effective for other Sales Professionals.

Although many selling concepts are elementary and work universally, I adopt an attitude that the employment and effectiveness of selling techniques is personal. Each individual Sales Professional must use what works for them.

You employ what works for you.

The following pages will not only provide you with new insight into the major reason(s) why you may not be closing like you should, but will also provide you with exercises to perform that will tear down the mental wall that is blocking you from feeling comfortable about closing. Armed with this knowledge, you will start closing more, and you will generate more Sales.

TWO

I'LL RENT THAT

Sometimes, we want to make things more complicated than what they are. It is normal to take an issue of significance and feel the need to assign some greater, philosophical meaning to it. We want to go beyond the obvious and search for the profound. It seems to be a human nature to overanalyze things sometimes.

On the flip side, as opposed to overanalyzing things, sometimes we just simply buy into some belief that another person presents to us. We just go along with their belief, simply because at that particular time it sounds "good enough for us". Particularly on issues we probably couldn't prove anyway, we have little or no desire to investigate the issue and arise our own view, so we simply say that we are "easy" and use the cliché, "I'll go along with that," or, "I'm with you."

For decades, the answer to the question, "Why don't Sales Professionals close?" was because they have a "fear of rejection". When I heard that, I just went along with it. Although it made some sense to me, at the gut level, something about it never fully registered with me.

I was just starting my selling career the first time I heard the "fear of rejection" concept. I did not have very much experience when I first heard it, and since I had no other view to replace it with, I just "went along with it".

For many years, at every Sales Seminar I attended, when the speaker approached the subject of why Sales Professionals don't close, I anticipated the speaker presenting the "fear of rejection" as the answer. As I mentioned earlier, I was privileged to have learned from numerous trainers – the absolute best in the business.

The top trainers each had their individual twist on the basic, fundamental selling strategies, but the number one reason preventing Sales Professionals from closing was universally presented in the same language. The top trainers all recited the same reason for what was the largest obstacle to overcome at closing: the "fear of rejection".

I really didn't care much that the "fear of rejection" seemed superficial during my 20-year tenure selling big-tickets. But when my Personal Development Company expanded, I developed an appetite for more insight into this alleged myth of the fear of closing.

I found it.

Before I share the following information, I want to assert that I am not fully enlightened with the wisdom of knowing what *every* Sales Professional thinks.

Everyone in my circle tells me that they appreciate my non-assuming approach. And as I mentioned earlier, I have evaluated thousands of Sales Professionals. However, I may not have spoken to *you*. If I have not spoken to you, I don't know what *your* thoughts are and why *you* might not be closing like *you* should.

Everyone is different. Although certain selling strategies apply universally, such as "Make your customer feel comfortable", the specific manner in which each Sales Professional accomplishes that task depends entirely on the individual Sales Professional's personality.

Let's examine more closely the fear of rejection.

The way I see it, many fears are not about the action itself, but what the *imagined results* would be. For example, for me, the fear of heights was about *the fear of falling*. When I looked out tall buildings, my fear was the picture of me falling. My heart would race uncontrollably. It was all in my mind. It was the *imagined results* that I feared.

Going down the list of fears, you can view them from the *imagined result* of the fear. Fear of the dark… translates into "something might be there that you can't see and it might hurt you". It's not so much the dark itself, but the imagined result of the action of going into the dark that is feared.

Clearly, it goes without saying that you are not afraid of the words, "Do you want to buy it?"

To put that thought to bed: right now, say out loud, "Do you want to buy it?"

Without a doubt, it is not those few words that you fear. What you really fear is the *imagined result* of asking those few words.

This is what you want to identify and work through.

The exercise below will identify your *imagined results* and determine your specific fear about closing. As opposed to having someone inform you of what your fears are, you will achieve better quality results by conducting the exercise yourself, for two reasons:

1. You know yourself better than anyone else.

2. As opposed to having someone else inform you of what your fears are, attaining the answer as a result of your own internal inquiry bestows power to the answer. You will believe *you*.

Upon completion of this exercise below, you will identify your fear(s) of why you are not closing like you should. Pause for a moment and reach deep into your inner feelings, so you can identify your true fear of the *imagined results*.

The Myth of the Fear of Rejection

Imagine what would happen if I asked them to buy

<table>
<tr><td>**Good**
(I'll help get you started)</td><td>**Bad**</td></tr>
<tr><td>1. They would buy</td><td>1.</td></tr>
<tr><td>2. I could decide on how to spend the commission money</td><td></td></tr>
<tr><td>3. This sale would get my boss off my back</td><td></td></tr>
<tr><td>4. I would make a new friend</td><td></td></tr>
<tr><td>5. I could call(text) everyone and tell them I sold one</td><td></td></tr>
<tr><td>6. They might need to sleep on it, so I could get an appointment for them to revisit</td><td></td></tr>
<tr><td>7. They might say no. I could find out if anything was preventing them from moving forward and have an opportunity to help resolve it...</td><td></td></tr>
<tr><td>8.</td><td></td></tr>
</table>

Sometimes, we mistrust ease and clarity. We push the obvious aside looking for the profound. Yes, I intended you to chuckle inside as you completed this exercise and read my answers which were only on the good side and left the bad side blank. If you took this as dead serious, that's O.K. too. You are now focused on *you* and *your* thoughts about closing – the focus of this book.

Now you are focused on an issue that will make a profound change in your life. Close more - sell more. More *closed* deals is the "cure all".

Also, it is safe to say here that the myth of the "fear of rejection" is busted.

In the above exercise, I did not list anything to help you with in the bad column. Across North America, thousands of Sales Professionals have shared their thoughts with me about what they would put in the bad column. It took many years of research to bust the fear of rejection myth.

Why Sales Professionals do not close, and more importantly, what to do about it, is a subject that I feel is most beneficial to you, especially in challenging economic times.

I believe in the power of humor. I have found that delivering a serious point with humor and clarity provides the greatest results. There are several illustrations to bust the myth about the fear of rejection in a humorous way.

The following is one of my favorites.

The Myth of the Fear of Rejection

"All I did was tell 'em I wanted to think about it."

Clearly, there are no physical consequences as a result of a customer rejecting your offer to buy. No debate is required to establish that there is nothing to be afraid of about closing - *except for thoughts manufactured in the Sales Professional's mind*. Controlling those thoughts requires some awareness and mental conditioning.

The following pages will raise your level of awareness about closing and will be the beginning of a mental conditioning program that will get your closing beliefs and attitudes "mentally fit".

COMEDY RELIEF

When I have reservations about something – a "fear" – and those thoughts are blocking my success, what works for me is to envision the worst consequence imaginable about that fear. In other words, I picture my *imagined result* of the action I fear. Then, I anchor in my mind a comical picture to that worst-case scenario. When I think of that scenario, the anchored memory is recalled…the humorous one… and the fear melts away.

For me, *owning the feeling* of the fear allows me to *control it.*

I will share with you a personal example of this. When I launched my Sales Training Company in 1996, my fear of public speaking was quite officious. I wanted to contribute to the success of others, and that realm of possibility meant public speaking. My fear was definitely blocking my success. I was petrified at just thinking about speaking to a large group of people.

I had a physical handicap from ages 5-17 years old. During the three identity-building stages of 4-6, 10-12, and early adulthood, I was made fun of. Not only did the outside world laugh at me, but every morning and every night I looked in the mirror and confirmed that something was wrong with me. This definitely damaged my self-image. But at age 17, the handicap was corrected. So why then, 20-30 years later, did those thoughts of not being good enough still show up? It's simply how the mind works, and that is another book.

I want to stay focused here on the fact that I recognized that my perceived fear was not in the physical act itself of speaking in front of people. Well beyond the *physical act* of standing in front of a group of people and speaking was the *mental thought* about it. It was my *imagined result* that was causing my fear.

So, just like you, I did the good/bad exercise.

Listing on paper the anticipated good and bad imagined results about a scenario allows an individual to organize and closely examine their fear and see that it is only their mental thought about it. In others words, identify the specific imagined result causing the fear. Once you do that - change can happen.

It really does work.

In my self-inquiry about my fear of public speaking, I probed further into understanding exactly what I was afraid of. I clearly identified and defined what that fear was. I found that at the core of my inner fear of speaking to a large group of people was that people would do to me what I saw them do to other key-note speakers at some events I had attended.

The thought that I isolated was imagining that while I was speaking to a group, some of the people were having side conversations at their tables. Even worse, some were laughing with each other, as if they had no regard for what I was saying. This was because of recalled memories of those damaged self-identity years.

There was another view about public speaking as well.

In some ways, I will admit that I am old school. In my opinion, when a speaker is in front of a group talking, I believe that out of respect for the speaker, there should not be any side conversations. It seems that the side conversations appear to be getting worse. It is probably a reflection of our current, ego-driven culture in this country. I have not attended enough events abroad to have an opinion of what happens in other countries; I hope it is better.

At any rate, as a result of my self-inquiry, I discovered that I had mislabeled my fear of public speaking. It was the specific, *imagined results* of public speaking – owning the view of being treated disrespectfully is what I feared.

I owned that view too long. It was time for me to discard that view and rent another one. I owe my awareness of the consequences of owning views about things that are not reality to an organization called Landmark Education.

Landmark Education is an organization that does work all over the world. Their focus is to bring awareness to people about how their mind works. What they do is not offered in our country's public education system. Landmark Education has opened an entire new realm of possibility for me by bringing awareness about the way the human mind operates, and how it is normal for an individual to live in the response of one's past and present *interpretation* of reality. In addition, one can limit the future possibilities based entirely on one's imagined or expected future events.

Without getting off the focus of this book, let's make the distinction of my imagined results of public speaking versus reality, and that my owning the view that people would be disrespectful was a mental wall blocking my success.

The first clue about the false pretense in my view is the phrase *imagined results*. It was one view of many about what *might* happen when I spoke to a large group. We could make up a long list of possibilities, a long list of imagined results about what could happen if I spoke to a large group of people. You don't have to stop at one reason or view; you can be creative and make a long list.

And whichever reason you choose – you're right!

As opposed to just living in the present moment, inventing what I wanted my future to be and living in that intention, I limited my success by turning down lucrative offers – all based on the worst I *imagined* might happen!

Just as easily, I can imagine the large group giving me a standing ovation!

That mental picture of a standing ovation is just as easy to manufacture and anchor as picturing people talking at their tables. I might as well throw in someone sitting there in the front row texting while I'm talking – makes perfect sense to me.

The bottom line, what I want you to walk away with here, is that *my view*…was only a thought *inside my head.* It was my view – only one view of which there were multiple choices of views to choose from. This awareness caused me to start a new cliché. Instead of saying "I'll buy that", I now say "I'll rent that" when it comes time to choose a view.

The important thing here is that life's circumstances present a multiple choice of views; you choose *one* of those *multiple choices* and consider that you are renting it. If that one view you choose does not produce beneficial results – rent another one.

Clearly, instead of the view that people show no respect by talking when a speaker is talking, another view to choose is the view that the speaker gets paid whether the people listen or not! The listeners are the beneficiaries of the information that the speaker delivers. So goes the saying:

"You can only help those that help themselves."

Further mental conditioning that I did to conquer my fear about public speaking was to picture the worst-case scenario, which for me was to get no respect, or even be laughed at. I pictured getting up in front of a large group of people, and looking at all of them talking at their tables and paying no attention to me. I owned the feeling of standing there as that was happening.

"...and after years of research I found..."

I *owned the feeling* of being laughed at by a large group of people. It wasn't all that bad. I laughed with them. After finding humor in that scenario, I thought of another view.

As I laughed at that mental picture, I rented the view that the poor souls talking and laughing at their tables were being held hostage by their egos. The ego was preventing them from absorbing the material that would prove beneficial to their greater success. As a result, those people were going to remain stuck at their current level of achievement where their egos could toy with them.

The ego has a sick sense of humor. Their egos could convince them that they didn't have enough stuff, while at the same time limiting their success. Ironically, it was the ego that was telling them to go get more stuff, yet it was preventing them from getting it!

I had a deep feeling of empathy for those people and I felt compelled to help those poor souls in the group that were being held hostage by their egos. I wanted to enlighten them to a better life. I wanted to break them free of the limitations they were victim to, and break them out of the small mental boxes they were forced to exist in.

It's just another view for rent.

Some time ago, I began to feel compassion for the unfortunate people whose egos bully their intellect. I felt the desire to help them. I know the ego is strong; I wrestle many thoughts away from mine on a constant basis. When I strangle my ego and suppress it, I am able to transform that limiting, negative energy into an abundant amount of positive energy.

Living in positive energy with creative-intention and contribution raises my spirit. I feel uplifted. I have power. I have inner peace. I enjoy sharing this breakthrough with others and have dedicated the rest of my life to it. My forthcoming book, entitled Attract vs. Attack, is about transcending the ego from sabotage to success. It's about how to reset negative, ego-based goals that only provide short-lived satisfaction, to positive, creative goals of contribution that are self-fulfilling and everlasting.

The conclusion to my self-inquiry about my fear of public speaking was that I would change my view and speak to larger groups. I would speak to large groups, gratefully owning the wisdom about people and the daily challenges of what influences their thoughts. Contrary to my intention of wanting to be the procuring cause for *everyone* in the group to enjoy their life to the fullest extent possible, I accepted the possibility that I just might not move, touch or inspire *every* person in *every* group. So goes the saying: "You can't please everyone."

Sharing this with you will help you understand how it translates to your view of not closing. You no longer have to fear your "imagined results" of closing. You can conquer that thought.

Whether you think you can become a great closer or not…either way, you're right.

FEAR BUDDIES

We have acknowledged the imagined fear that Sales Professionals may have, but I have not yet mentioned another person facing fear – *the customer.* Your customer has their own fear. They fear different things at different times throughout their buying process.

Calming their fear will allow you to close more deals. In addition, if you remain focused on your customer throughout the process, you might recognize the customer going through buyer's remorse. By using your insight to the wants and needs of your customer, you can calm their fear.

Even in prosperous economic times, consumers still fear big-ticket Sales. Your product or service could not only be conceived of as a good chunk of money to them, but also the consequences of their purchase could have a profound effect on their life.

They can have fear about several different things. Examples are: your company's service after the sale, the longevity of the product, whether or not they are getting the best value. These are just a few fears that may arise during their shopping process.

You can take your company's product or service out of the equation and your customer may still be dealing with fear about other issues. For example, if you are selling real estate, you may have performed your "A Game" presentation and found the perfect home for your customers, but they might have fears about other issues that are far beyond your control.

Maybe your customer fears that their job or business is not all that secure. Here they are, out looking at homes, yet when confronted with the decision to actually purchase, this fear surfaces – and they don't buy. They fall off their shopping process for a while, all because an *imagined result* surfaced.

The point is this: your customers are faced with their own "imagined results" – their own fears about things - outside of you.

Your customers may simply not understand the whole process of buying your product. This falls into the category of the "fear of the unknown". This fear may sound like it has no significance, but keep in mind some basic human natures.

People take the least path of resistance. If they have to work hard with you to get all the facts they need, while your competitor lays it out for them and makes the process sound simple and fun – guess who gets the sale: your competitor.

We could venture here into the subject matter of how much you – the Sales Professional – can make the difference. I have seen thousands of big-ticket Sales Presentations. After evaluating so many in the same day or in the same week, there definitely develops a cloud of redundancy.

For example, have you ever taken a few days and gone to a new city where you might relocate to, and during those few days looked at 6-8 homebuilders? Perhaps you looked in a few surrounding cities of the target area that you wanted to live. How many times did you hear from the homebuilders that you're "in the best school district"? Put it this way; I have looked at homebuilders from San Diego to Seattle, from Miami to Maryland, and a lot of places in between – 68 major US cities – and every one of the builders mentioned that they were in a great school district.

Several other platitudes were boldly spoken, as if they were exclusives.

Examples were: 'Builder of the Year' – almost all builders were during some given year; 'excellent customer survey scores' and 'great customer service after the sale'; a 'great warranty program'…etc.

You hear very similar stories all across America. No matter what product or service you are selling… everyone in your business is singing the same song you are.

I am not saying that you shouldn't bother mentioning any of the above. The point is this: don't think that saying "great customer service" is a tangible that your customer will perceive as the difference maker. I recognize that you may be really excited about your service. And if you have arrived at the level of enlightenment where service is just about the only thing that can separate you from your competitors, and you heavily invest your efforts to achieve better customer service – bravo!

The point to walk away with is that just simply stating you have great customer service is not enough. Others will claim the same. And although their claims may be unsubstantiated, they will still sound the same as yours. You have to support your claim. Invest the proper time to convey your service distinctions – it deserves far more than "we have great service".

I want you to walk away with the fact that you – the Sales Professional – can make the difference in your customer's decision. Even when you are at a disadvantage with product, price, or timing – you can still win.

I had a new home customer tell me that they liked another builder's floor plan better than mine because the other floor plan had a great place to display their grand piano. I couldn't help them with that. My home design could not be adjusted at a cost-effective level to get it similar to the other builder's floor plan. But they bought from me because they liked me better; they really did not like the other builder's Sales Professional.

To close out this thought, I want you to look at the big picture here. Your job as a Sales Professional is to reduce - if not eliminate entirely - your *customer's fear(s)*. You want to eliminate all of the fear that is within your power to eliminate, because there may be some fear over which you have no influence.

In fact, many customers do not advertise their inner fears.

You need to be the strong one. You lead and they will follow. You not only make buying from you simple – make it fun as well. Make the customer see that doing business with you will be a pleasure, and that they will be much better off with you as their Sales Professional because you really care and you are a pleasure to be around.

You make their day.

So often, we complain about how little service we get anymore. Well, you are in control of that. One Sales Professional at a time will change the world of customer service.

One at a time.

A very short story about how you can change the world one person at a time:

My son's Varsity football team had an attitude challenge. They lost their first six straight games. The seniors were down and depressed. For many on the team, this was their last time playing pad football. Think about it; nearly all sports – basketball, baseball, tennis etc. – can be played somewhere as an adult. But pad football is very unique in the fact that you don't go down to the local park and play pad football.

The seniors on my son's team were aware that this was their last season - and they lost their first 6 games in a row! They doubted that they would go to the playoffs. In order to go, they had to win out the rest of the season.

My son was a Team Leader…and a well-respected star player. He asked me what to do about the somber mood of the team. He had no idea how to turn his team spirit around because nearly all of the players were depressed. I gave him a suggestion.

I spelled it out this way. I explained that the first thing he wanted to do was get his best ally, one player on his side, and implement this plan. I explained that he should get one player to buy into his effort of turning the team spirit around. Once he had his best ally on board, now there were two of them. They each would go get one more player to come on board. Then they had 4, and so on.

In other words, my son would approach the entire team as individual players. I explained that he should listen to all that they had to say…don't make them wrong for their thoughts; respect their thoughts and have empathy – after all, he could understand; he was one of them.

My son took me up on that idea – and the team turned around. They made the playoffs!

My point here is for you to walk away with the power of one person at a time will make the difference. You can change the world – one person at a time.

When we face global issues, we can sometimes wonder, "How will there be any change when we as individuals can only do so much?" That's right; as an individual, alone, we can only do so much...but who we move, touch and inspire – moves, touches and inspires others, and so on.

There is great power in word of mouth. It's far better than any external advertisement because it is transferred from one individual's heart to another. Personal transfer of emotion from one person to another runs much deeper than the influence of any advertisement.

What emotions about your product or service are you transferring to your customers? You own the feeling first, then convey it to them. They see their possibilities through you.

Put your fear aside – and help them with theirs!

I invite you to make your self-inquiry about your view of why you might not be closing like you should. As you probe to isolate your specific thoughts about not closing, be honest with yourself about the fact that you aren't King Closer of planet Earth. Be humble enough, and accept that if an alien recruiter for Sales Professionals came from another galaxy and landed on Earth asking, "Who is the best closer of all the humans?" – accept that you wouldn't get that call (or text).

In other words, give your ego a tranquilizer and allow your intellect to absorb the material that follows. This is all about *you*, and living your life to the fullest.

Clearly, we have busted the myth of "fear of rejection". There is no physical consequence of your customer not accepting your generous offer to purchase. In fact, you see where your customer is the one that can be faced with fears. Every human being is faced with their *imagined results*.

Clearly, your challenge is all mental. The following chapters will reveal some reasons why you might not be closing like you want to.

Each of the reasons that you will learn about are common to many other Sales Professionals across North America. *You are not alone* in wanting to break down the mental block that prevents people from closing. You no longer have to own the view that you have a mental block about closing. Instead, right now you can rent the view that after reading this book, you will have the insight to close with ease.

Trust the ease and clarity with which this information is delivered. Allow your intellect to absorb this material – being a great closer already exists in you; you just have to remove the obstacles that are in your way.

Chapter Highlights

Be aware that your view is not the only view because no matter what the circumstance, there will be a multiple choice of "views" from which to choose.

Constantly access how much your view costs you, and possibly trade it for one less costly.

Make clear distinctions between your "imagined results" and reality.

As opposed to setting your mind on "autopilot" and allowing it to automatically respond to its interpretations of reality - make conscious choices of response.

THREE

CLOSE DEFINED

For the intent and purposes as it will be used in this book, let's make a clear distinction of the definition of "closing". You would think this would not be necessary, but if you had seen what I have, you would feel compelled to make this distinction — to define 'closing'.

When I reference closing, what I mean is that a Sales Professional has closed — has *asked* for the sale - when the Sales Professional asks the customer to move forward and remove the specific product out of the "for sale" column in the company's books, and move it into the "sold" column. In other words, the specific product is no longer available for sale to anyone else…it is sold, gone, taken…no one else can buy it at that particular point in time…period.

The above closing scenario is for specific, tangible products; one-of-a-kind home, specific car, etc. For other things that can be ordered, or services that can be duplicated — for example, the same type of life insurance policy that can be sold to different people all day – a close is when the Sales Agent asks the client to move forward with a purchase and acknowledges the purchase with a written agreement. And if it is company policy, the written agreement is accompanied with a financial instrument. This closes the deal.

From another perspective, under the definition used in this book, look at what is not a close. The following statements and questions are not closing statements and questions:

> When will you be making a decision?

> What do you think?

> Do you like it?

> Do you have any other questions?

It is easy to see that the above questions do not require the customer to take any *specific action to proceed with a purchase at that time*. The above are only questions – none are "a close".

Yet, some Sales Professionals act as if they are closes – no, I'm not trying to be funny. I *can* be funny, and this is *not* a joke.

Let's make a clear distinction here. Let's look at what explaining the buying process vs. closing is. Many Sales Professionals who are climbing the ladder of Sales Education are learning the distinction of what explaining "*how to*" buy is, compared to asking the customer to "*buy it*".

An explanation is just that, an *explanation*. It goes something like this:

> If you wanted to move forward, this is what you would do. You would_____.
> (Explain what they need to do, sign the agreement, show me the money, etc.)

After the explanation of "how to" buy it, there might be an explanation of what the next steps taken would be after they buy it. For example, after buying a new home you might meet the builder, go to the mortgage company, and perhaps go to the design center, etc. (You would probably ask them to go to the mortgage company first.)

Another buying process might be that the Sales Professional needs to initiate an ordering process on what was purchased. Perhaps the way to buy in this scenario is leave an initial deposit, and the balance is due when you take delivery of the merchandise. Obviously, companies have different point-of-sale polices.

The distinction to be made here is that after a simple *explanation* of the process of "how to" buy it, the customer does not need to take any action at all. In essence, after being informed on what to do if they wanted to buy it, the customer could just sit or stand there looking at the Sales Professional - and say nothing.

I have many times.

Perhaps you have as well.

No response is required after listening to an explanation about "how to" buy it. You could answer, "Oh, I see," or a number of other similar responses, none of which would commit you to *buying it.*

Some Sales Professionals, especially newbies, are stuck on the idea that since they *explained* that a deposit is required in order to "take it off the market", they must have closed. In reality, they only explained *how* to take it off the market. They did not ask the customer to actually take it off the market.

They were only one sentence away from closing.

It is amazing the difference that a question can make as opposed to an explanation.

How about this one:

"Will you marry me?"

You can *explain* about it all you want to, or have someone explain to you all about marriage. And you can talk all day about "how to" get married, or what you would do after you got married. But actually being *asked* the question "Will you marry me?" is quite different. It requires an action from the person asked.

Asking someone to buy something is very similar to asking someone to get married. The questions are similar, but the answers you get are a little different.

After asking customers to buy, I've heard customers say that they wanted to "look around a little more" – but I have not heard of any cases where someone that was asked to get married answered, "I want look around a little more."

You get the point. We have made a clear distinction between explaining "how to," as opposed to "asking to."

Now that closing is crystal clear, let's get to it. Let's identify and conquer the reasons why you aren't.

FOUR

HALF-BAKED

You have probably dealt with a personal issue, something that you had to make a decision about, and at the time, you felt that the decision you were going to make would have a profound impact on your life. Getting married, taking a certain job, where to live – all good examples of issues you might have faced that required critical thinking.

In wrestling with making your decision, you probably thought about it while you drove your car, while you were in the shower, before you went to bed… sometimes it might have showed up as soon as you opened your eyes in the morning. You kept asking yourself, "What should I do?"

Your thought processes on that particular issue consumed your normal motivations and overwhelmed your everyday life. Then, finally, you made a decision. You chose what to do. Afterwards, sometime later, you realized that it really wasn't that big of a deal after all. In fact, the deciding factors may have been quite clear, but you drug out the process by throwing way too much into it.

Sometimes, we mistrust ease and clarity.

Over the years, I saw a shift in the dynamics of the most widely accepted fundamental and universal selling strategy. This fundamental strategy is broken down into components known as the greeting, qualifying, demonstrating, and closing.

The first pyramid of this selling strategy placed the greatest emphasis on the closing. In other words, the way I learned it – which goes back to the late 1970s – was that a Sales Professional greeted the customer, learned their needs and wants, demonstrated the product, and then, at the end of the presentation, the Sales Professional pulled out their bag of 101 closes and used one. If they said no, you found out why…sold a little more…and pulled another close out of the bag.

In other words, you were armed with an arsenal of closes. The strategy called for less emphasis on the greeting and greater emphasis on the closing.

That strategy was employed for quite some time. Then, one day in the early '90s, someone turned that strategy upside down and presented the idea that the greatest emphasis should *not* be on the closing. Instead, they sold the idea that the new strategy should require greater emphasis on the greeting and relationship building, and that less emphasis was required on the closing.

The 'new' thinking was that if you put more emphasis on establishing a relationship with the customer and presenting what they wanted *their way*, then at closing you would be in a logical, make-sense place, and there wouldn't be any use for a "101 Closes". Just throw that book away.

They sold this concept well.

Countless books were written in the '90s on "Relationship Selling" and the pyramid was printed upside down and passed around. This selling style gained popularity. It seemed like in no time that the consensus honored "Relationship Selling" as the best selling strategy.

When you look at this major shift in selling strategy, it is radical – but very simple. This is the point that I want you to get – *it is really very simple*. What appeared to be a radical change in strategy was in reality no real challenge in execution. Gee...make a friend. How hard was that?

The following is the first reason why you might not be closing. I created two metaphors for you to picture this concept and better understand it.

First, imagine that your customer walks into your office with a box of pieces to a puzzle. Normally, the puzzle box has a picture on it. However, in this case, there is no picture. Instead, the customer must describe the picture to you, so you have to ask questions.

It's called...*qualifying*.

That is why the Sales Gurus have been preaching for years that you have to make people feel comfortable and establish rapport in your greeting – so your customer will open up to you and describe their picture in great detail, so you stand a better chance in putting it together.

The better the qualifying, the better chance you have. Let me explain further. You really need to get this.

Let's say that you ask a qualifying question like "What kind of picture is it?" This is the equivalent of , "What are you looking for?"

The customer answers, "My picture is a scenery picture."

Although this answer, "a scenery picture", is only the beginning, countless Sales Professionals make the mistake of considering it the end. The Sales Professional mistakenly starts into their presentation with only a small amount of description which is not significant enough.

You *could* start building the puzzle, but with so many variables and different pictures of scenery, you would be quite challenged, to say the least, in completing your project anytime soon. Plus, many customers don't even know what their picture looks like…they can't even describe it themselves!

That's why you qualify.

The more questions you ask, the more personal and specific information you get from your customer, the better you can work together. Not only will you ask the customer for specifics about "what" the picture is, but as a seasoned Sales Professional, you will graduate to asking beyond the "what" questions and also ask the customer to describe "why" they like it.

The "what" answers provide you with the physical "facts and features". The "why" answers will provide you with the emotional reasons that inspire and motivate the customer's desire to own that picture.

Your job as a Sales Professional is not only to influence the customer to fall in love with the picture of the puzzle that you and the customer are putting together, but if you're good, the customer will believe that it was the picture that *they* came up with – not you.

This is the difference between *order-taking* and *selling*.

If you're not already doing this, the day you start selling to the buyer's emotions is the day your Sales career will become easier and more fun, and your Sales results will reach their fullest potential. You will perform more "A" game presentations, and you will consistently be at the top of your game. You'll notice a dramatic increase in your income when you *sell* as opposed to taking orders.

But let's get back to the point about you and your customer putting together their puzzle.

Let's say that you have asked some general qualifying questions or "overview" questions as opposed to getting into the specifics – then it would be natural and logical that your presentation would mirror your collected answers. In other words, your presentation would be an "overview".

Then, how could you close?

Most Sales Professionals wouldn't, because they would not feel comfortable – *it just wouldn't feel right.*

For any Sales Professional that would try, the position they are in is one of "Trust Me". In essence, the close would be, in concept, one where the picture is not complete. You might see the gist of it, so the Sales Professional is in a position of asking the customer to trust the Sales Professional that the picture will turn out like the one the customer has in their mind.

In a world that is dominated by living in fear, *trust* has become a scarce commodity.

If given the choice, which every Sales Professional has when they begin to put the puzzle together with their customer, why leave the position of closing to one where you are literally forcing the customer to throw their money at you in hopes that it will all somehow work out?

Those people buy today and cancel tomorrow.

Another way to illustrate this point is by looking at using a recipe to make something. It's always the "special ingredients" that make it distinct. Say, for example, you go to a chili cook-off event. You taste all of the different chilies. It's the "ingredients" that make the difference – the ingredients and the recipe determine the winner!

Let's follow through with this thought. Imagine watching someone baking a cake. They pour all of the ingredients into a bowl. Next, they mix the ingredients. Then, they pour the cake mix into a baking pan and put it in the oven. Let's say that the recipe called for baking the cake for 40 minutes, so they set the oven timer for 40 minutes.

But after baking it for only 20 minutes, they pull it out of the oven.

In a very uncomfortable manner, they ask you if you want to buy it.

You probably wouldn't buy the cake, would you?

Imagine that the person baking the cake is a Sales Professional.

The Sales Professional is faced with a major reason why they can't ask you to buy the cake. They wouldn't feel comfortable asking you to buy the cake simply because – it was only half-baked!

Let's translate this into plain, selling English. Again, I will remind you and reemphasize that simple is good. Ease and clarity works.

Let's say that whatever you are selling requires a *planned Sales Presentation* – equivalent to a baking recipe. Instead of making a sale, we'll call it the recipe to *bake a sale*.

Let's revisit the most universal, yet simple, model of selling strategy - the greeting, qualifying, demonstrating and closing strategy. Within the components of this strategy are the *ingredients* to bake the sale.

You have ingredients, things to say and do along the way through your planned presentation. For example, you use different ingredients in your greeting to establish rapport with your customer. The ingredients called for might be for you to introduce yourself, get your customer's name, make small talk before starting into business, be focused on them, have good eye-contact, etc.

None of those ingredients should be left out. The greeting turns out great when you include all of the ingredients.

Beyond the greeting, the other parts of the *planned presentation* - the qualifying, demonstration and closing - each have *ingredients* as well.

It is important to acknowledge that *all* of the ingredients are necessary to bake a sale. The recipe calls for a complete, planned presentation by following the recipe using *all* of the ingredients.

Similar to not feeling comfortable in asking someone to buy a cake that you only half-baked, you wouldn't feel comfortable asking someone to buy your product at the end of your presentation if the presentation was only halfway done.

"Want to try some?"

Let me add to what I mentioned earlier: I have found that ease, clarity and *humor* provide the greatest results.

This half-baked insight requires a self-inquiry with focus on your planned presentation. Perhaps one mental block that you have about closing is that you are not in a *comfortable* position to close. You may have left out some of the ingredients – so you just don't feel comfortable to close.

You want to uncover any habits that you have developed which short-change, or leave out, some of the ingredients that make an "A Game" presentation.

Normally, the longer a Sales Professional does the same presentation, the more the possibility increases that they have developed a bad habit somewhere. The seasoned professional wants to get through it – "bake it" faster. The old pros learn how to make a "fast food" version of their presentation.

If you want living proof that the "must include all of the ingredients" theory works – just watch a newbie. Brand new Sales Professionals don't know any better, and they just do the entire presentation – at least for a while. The old pros watch new Sales Professionals use all of the ingredients in the recipe and do everything the presentation calls for to make the sale – and sure enough, they make one.

The fact is, countless old pros have witnessed new Sales Professionals make Sales right in front of them, and afterwards, the old pros acknowledge the new Salesperson's "not knowing any better" as the reason why the new Sales Professional sold one.

The old pro makes it sound as if it were an accident!

The most common bad habit I have seen with old pros is that they raise the baking temperature and shorten the baking time. The old pros "turn up the heat" and shorten the bake time by cutting the time of their presentation short. That's because the ego convinces them that they *know* the *best ingredients* to use, because they are seasoned Sales Professionals, so they can concoct their own recipe.

And what is incredible but true, is that similar to leaving out just *one ingredient* when baking a cake, or simply raising the heat and shortening the baking time, leaving out one small ingredient of the Sales Presentation, or raising the heat or cutting the presentation time short, will deliver non-desirable results.

If you self-reflect, you may identify ingredients in your Sales Presentation that you are not performing completely. I will help get your thought process started and then you will further reflect on your Sales Presentation.

Starting with your greeting, are you performing all of the ingredients that make a great greeting? Review what that recipe calls for:

Smile; give a warm, friendly welcome

Introduction – give your name and get their name

Focus; have great eye-contact

Show a genuine interest in your customer

Small talk before starting into business

What else?

Clearly, depending on what you are selling, there are variables in the recipe of your greeting, as well as the rest of your *planned presentation*. You know what they are – if you don't, put this book down and find out.

I believe that you adjust your recipe to the taste of your customers. I am not covering that material in this book. Clearly, you would not ask a customer to buy your cake that you just baked with sugar – if they were diabetic!

You know by now that you need to speak to your customers in their world of listening. Remember, when you're selling - it's all about them.

A-LA-CART

Remember that people buy on *emotion* and justify with *logic*. Both need to happen to increase your chances to make the sale. Examine your Sales Presentation and see if your focus is just on *one* or the *other.*

The most common mistake that most Sales Professionals make is to only emphasize the facts and features that fall in the "justify buying it". Most Sales Trainers would label this "feature dumping". The customer is hammered with features, but their *emotion* is not tickled on *owning* the feature. The customer just follows along. If tested, the customer might recall 10% - 20% of your presentation.

How long did it take you to remember it? More than once.

Non-emotional, facts-and-features-only presentations can actually cause a customer to *not* buy from you. Even worse, a feature-only presentation may kick the customer into a "more features for the lowest price" shopping mode. After leaving your boring pile of facts, they go somewhere else – to your competitor.

At one of your competitors, your customer gets tired of looking. Their emotions are tickled and they buy; whether their emotions were tickled by the other Sales Professional ,or generated by the customer – either way you've lost another sale. They got tired and laid-down for the competitor.

Sometimes, people are sold without the Sales Professional working very hard. In my time, we referred to these easy Sales as "slam-dunks", "floor pops", or "lay-downs" – maybe you've had one or two of those. These type of Sales can be euphoric in nature, but you can't earn a living from them.

The other common mistake made by many Sales Professionals is the opposite of a boring, robotic, facts/features-only presentation; on the flip side, I have seen countless Sales Presentations where the Sales Professional went overboard in establishing rapport. They displayed a genuine interest in me, and I couldn't help but like them. They went out of their way to be "friendly". I have really had fun watching some Sales Presentations.

If I were to choose which Sales Professional to buy from, either the boring facts-and-features person vs. the bubbly, friendly, gotta-love-em person, I'd choose the latter. Better bubbly than bored is my personal preference.

But clearly, selling in only one context alone, features or rapport – in other words, "a la cart" – will only allow for the easiest of Sales and your success will be limited.

By performing your planned presentation, using all of the ingredients and taking the amount of time called for in the recipe to bake the sale, at the end of your presentation you and your customers will be in a comfortable place to close.

COMPLETE THE FOLLOWING EXERCISE.

Perform a self-inquiry. See if you need to remember to include any ingredients that you might be leaving out. Make notes in the space provided or use a separate sheet of paper.

THE GREETING

I will make my greeting complete by including the following ingredients:

QUALIFYING

In my discovery of needs and wants I will make it complete by including these ingredients:

DEMONSTRATION

When I select something to demonstrate, and in the demonstration process, I will make it complete by including these ingredients:

CLOSING

When I close I will make it complete by including these ingredients:

I want you to walk away with the fact that you need to reflect on your presentation periodically. Hopefully, you found some ingredients to make sure you include, and that you are selling to your customer's emotions and helping them justify with logic.

The majority of the time, an ingredient is left out and the Sales Presentation is incomplete. Keep in mind, just like baking a cake, it only takes one ingredient left out to produce a less than desirable result.

Fill out the following chart and estimate how much you may have lost due to not following the recipe.

HALF-BAKED BOMBS

_____Number of times in the last 12 months I could not close because I half-baked the presentation and delivered a fast-food version

X

$_____ My average commission

= $_____ Total commissions I could have made in the last 12 months

To accurately evaluate your Sales Presentation you could hire a video shopping company to shop you. Don't tell anyone about it; just hire the company on your own and evaluate your Sales Presentation confidentially. Another option is to use a pocket recorder and record the audio portion of your presentation. I would rather see my body language and watch the video to get the full picture, but that's the view I rent.

Let's summarize the half-baked concept. It's simple; if the cake was made with all of the ingredients called for, and if it is baked at the temperature for the time called for, the cake will turn out. You will be in a much better position – and feel more comfortable - to ask someone to buy your cake.

The same goes for making a sale. You are in a much better position – and you will feel more comfortable to close at the end of a complete Sales Presentation - when you followed the recipe by including all of the ingredients and spent the proper amount of time with your customer.

Use all of the ingredients, follow the recipe, and generate more Sales.

The next chapter will reveal another possible reason that you may not be closing.

Chapter Highlights

By properly qualifying, you establish what picture of the puzzle you and your customer will put together.

Fully completing the puzzle together with your customer will leave you in a logical, make-sense position to close -- every time.

Seasoned Sales Professionals develop a bad habit of delivering a "fast-food" version of their presentation - they turn up the heat and reduce the baking time.

Constantly review your presentation to ensure that you are including all of the ingredients.

FIVE

FRIENDS

The concept of "Relationship Selling" really took off in the 1990s. With countless books written about it, and with all of the top trainers shifting their training workshops to it, Relationship Selling became the consensus in Sales strategy in the 1990s.

Over the years, it has been interesting, to say the least, watching how new thoughts about selling strategies become the norm. Some I have liked; some I haven't. Some ideas were introduced in such a manner that it appeared anyone could use them, regardless of their Sales skills. However, other ideas required in-depth clarification for even the old pros to employ.

Relationship Selling was a concept that definitely needed further elaboration than what was provided when it was originally introduced.

Overall, the relationship or "let's be friends" concept is a great thing, but in some cases, it has been grossly misunderstood. And, tragically but true, that misunderstanding has been guilty of limiting and even sabotaging Sales. As opposed to winning Sales contests, which it was intended to help do, Relationship Selling has made some Sales Professionals counterproductive.

Before I reveal the common misunderstanding about Relationship Selling, I want to shine some light on its true core concept – the *true* intention behind making the customer "your friend".

You make the customer your friend so they will open up to you – and show you how to *sell* them!

You may be limiting your Sales and not closing because of your misinterpretation of "Relationship Selling".

In this chapter, I will share with you not only how you might lose Sales from Relationship Selling, but more importantly, how to *close* with Relationship Selling. Relationship Selling is used throughout your presentation – and more than ever when you close.

We live in a culture where we feel unappreciated. People complain that their bosses do not acknowledge their efforts, their significant others don't acknowledge them, their children don't show any them appreciation, and their friends and family do not acknowledge them. People frequently voice their feelings of not being acknowledged.

No wonder the concept of Relationship Selling was embraced like none other. I wanted to buy something just so I could experience Relationship Selling – so I could feel acknowledged!

This insight will provide you with a huge advantage. *Acknowledgement* is what's at the core of Relationship Selling. We use to call it "make other people feel important". It was always an ingredient in the recipe to make a sale, but the amount called for increased in the 1990s. Someone relabeled "make other people feel important" as "Relationship Selling", and a paradigm shift occurred.

And yet, although the consensus has become that Relationship Selling is the best selling strategy, it seems that we get acknowledged by Sales Professionals less and less these days.

Something has gone wrong.

Remember the old concept "The customer is always right"? That's long gone. In our Western culture, we simply lack the desire to deal with people in a personal manner - even when they *are* right. Personal or professional, we don't want to hear people's stories, whether we're paid for it or not.

This about sums up our current cultural attitude on acknowledgement and personal service: I recently heard a motorcycle dealer's radio ad. I heard the owner of the dealership come on and say, "My name is _____. You can deal with me *personally*. Just *email me* at _____!"

What is that? Deal with me *personally* - by *email?* Wouldn't *personally* be…*in person?*

Now, let's identify why you may not be closing as a result of Relationship Selling.

As mentioned earlier, Relationship Selling was in the mainstream in the late 1990s and was well-practiced by the dawn of the new millennium. Right at the time of a booming economy, Sales Professionals just had to show up to work, be friendly, and take orders. The concept of making the customer "your friend" was not only learned by new Sales Professionals who were just entering their Sales career, but it was adopted by the old pros as well.

The "make a friend" concept really needed some clarity and focus on how to properly implement it into Sales Presentations. But, unfortunately, at the same time Relationship Selling was adopted by the mainstream, record Sales were being made. Sales Training was not the primary focus during a period where it was a challenge to deliver the goods that were already being sold, let alone putting great effort into how to sell more.

"Be a friend; take the order" became common business practice.

During the boom, Sales Professionals became passive – they became gracious hosts who believed that the proper selling strategy was to answer questions in a friendly manner, and develop a good *relationship* with the customer.

In other words, when the customer came in, instead of being the *driver* in the presentation – instead of asking questions and taking control while nurturing a good *relationship* – the Sales Professional switched seats. They got up from the driver's seat and became the passenger. They threw the keys to the customer and just went along for the ride.

During the boom, I witnessed many new Sales Professionals *only answer questions* in their presentation – not because they were defiant, not because they were lazy, but simply because *that's what they thought they were supposed to do*! This isn't speculation…I saw it first-hand.

It might be hard for you to imagine a Sales Presentation where the Sales Professional didn't ask one question. It might be a challenge to comprehend how that could even occur. For me, it's almost as hard as understanding how a mega-ship that weighs millions of tons can float – and I've seen just as many Sales Professionals not ask one question in a presentation as I have seen mega-ships float.

Hard to comprehend or not – both are common occurrences.

I have some compassion for new Sales Professionals who started their Sales career during the boom period and learned that "Sales" was about answering questions and taking orders. I have empathy for them for one simple reason: through no fault of their own, they had so many buyers coming at them that just taking the orders thrown at them was all they had to do.

Friends

Instead of being the "driver" in the Sales Presentation, by asking questions and taking control, new Sales Professionals threw the keys to the customer and thought they were supposed to be friendly by saying, "You drive; you go where you want to go, and I'd be happy to answer any questions that you might have along the way. That's what I'm here for."

However, that thought got stretched a little too far.

The Myth of the Fear of Rejection

**"Go ahead and make yourself at home;
if you need something, I'll be right here."**

As I mentioned earlier, I successfully sold big-tickets for over 20 years, and during my tenure, I became a professional student. I saw the top trainers and read countless books. In my opinion, no one ever really emphasized that the *real reason* you want customers to feel comfortable and relaxed is so you can sell them! It is easier to close them if you are in rapport!

People buy on *emotion* and justify with *logic*.

If the customer opens up to you, you can recognize the *emotional* needs and desires of the customer so you can *tickle* those emotional needs and tailor your presentation to them, and then allow them to *own* the facts and features.

From what I have seen, the *customers don't ask* the Sales Professional how the product is going to tickle their *emotional* needs – that's the Sales Professional's job.

The customer is only going to ask about the logical facts and features, and leaving it up to the customer to self-generate emotional satisfaction about your product is about like taking your mortgage payment to Las Vegas. You might win, but then again…

Normally, a Sales Professional who only answers questions will perform a dull, boring, read-the-instruction-manual type Sales Presentation that does not tickle any emotion.

Overall, no emotional attachment to the product = no sale.

How could a Sales Professional then *close* with the customer having *no emotional attachment* to the product?

It should be a crime – but some Sales Professionals try it anyway.

They ask for the sale after a boring, facts-only presentation – and that's why some Sales Professionals are perceived as "pushy".

The reason why some Used Car Salespeople are perceived as "pushy" is because they ask a closing question in the greeting. They ask something like, "Are you ready to make a deal today?" in the greeting. The customer has absolutely no *emotional* involvement yet and feels "pushed".

The potential car buyer needs to drive the car, get a feel for it, picture showing it off, etc., and acquire some emotional attachment about owning it first, before they will consider buying it.

So goes the recipe for *any* Sales Presentation.

Closing without emotional attachment is considered pushy, and we don't like it; as a result, we can be overly cautious that we don't seem pushy to our customers – understandable. But many Sales Professionals misunderstand what being perceived as "pushy" is.

Some Sales Professionals don't understand that if they performed their complete, planned presentation and used all of the ingredients in Relationship Selling properly, the customer would not see them as "pushy" at all. This is not in the same context as the Car Salesperson example above. Using a closing statement in the greeting like some Used Car Salespeople and performing an "A-Game" presentation are not remotely close.

This is where some light needs to be shed on the concept of Relationship Selling, and how the misconception of "be a friend" as a selling strategy can sabotage a sale. "Be a friend" does not mean be a gracious passenger and make yourself available only to answer the customer's questions.

Think about what happens when a customer has not shopped around enough to know what questions to ask. What happens? Very little is what happens; definitely slim-to-no-chance of a sale.

"Welcome, glad you stopped by.
No one has anything like our HNC4Q...want to buy it?"

Picture this humorous illustration:

Picture a Sales Presentation where the Sales Professional remained in an "answer questions" mode throughout the entire Sales Presentation.

At the end of this presentation, the customer doesn't know any more questions to ask; they have run out. After a pause from the customer, the Sales Professional asks...ready for it?..."Any other questions?"

Of course, the customer answers, "No, I can't think of any."

The Sales Professional closes with, or, better said, *finishes* with, "You have my card...if you have any questions, feel free to call me."

You can see the trap here. Watch out for the "gracious host, only answer questions" mode that sneaks in through the back door...it will cost you Sales.

Relationship Selling is not, "Make a friend and just answer questions."

Relationship Selling is, "Make a friend; allow them to relax, open up and let you know what their *emotional needs* are, so you can present your features to their emotional needs." You sell to their emotions and then justify with logic.

BUYING FRIENDS

There is another major way that Relationship Selling is misunderstood, and this way is calculated as the cause of more lost Sales than any other.

In this case, the Sales Professional is totally blocked from asking the customer to buy; in fact, the Sales Professional believes it would be *totally wrong* – *a bad thing* – if they asked the customer to buy.

Many Sales Professionals hit a mental block when it comes time to ask this one sentence – to ask this one little question, "Do you want to buy it?"

Many Sales Professionals believe that as a result of their asking that one little question, their *relationship* with their customer would *change*. Specifically, the Sales Professional thinks that all of their *rapport* would be *lost* with their customer.

Many Sales Professionals believe that their new-found "friend" would no longer consider them "friendly". So, in essence, they exchange their commission for their newfound friend.

When we probe a little deeper into the thoughts of Sales Professionals, we find that there are many Sales Professionals who believe that asking the customer to "buy it" would make them appear "pushy". Naturally, Sales Professionals don't want to be perceived as pushy. Many of them will try to ensure that their customers know that the Sales Professional is "just not like that".

Many Sales Professionals actually say in their presentation that they really aren't a *Salesperson.*

Ironically, at the perfect time to close, as opposed to saying that one little sentence – those few words – I have seen countless Sales Professionals attempt to remove themselves from being a "Salesperson". And as they mention this, they say it with an expression of disgust towards Sales Professionals.

When they hit the pillow at night are they really ashamed of what they do?

Or is this a misunderstanding of "Relationship Selling"?

I believe it's a misunderstanding of Relationship Selling, as well as not wanting to swim in the same pool with 'pushy Salespeople' – understandable.

However, if the Sales Professional owns the belief that because they did *not close,* the customer left in a state of "rapport" with them, and that the customer will ...are you ready for it? ...definitely "be-back" someday, then this belief has severe consequences. This misunderstanding will cause the Sales Professional to crash into a mental wall when it's time to close.

How much does this view cost you? Fill in the chart below.

COSTLY FRIENDS

_____ Total number of times in the last 12 months that I did not close because I did not want to appear 'pushy' and reduce the rapport I had with the customer

X

$_____ My average commission

= _____ Total commissions I could have made

There's more to this mistaken belief of not wanting to appear pushy and not wanting to reduce the rapport that the Sales Professional has worked so hard for.

To avoid being perceived as pushy, the Sales Professional experiences call reluctance when it's time to make follow-up calls. They own the belief that if they make the follow-up call to the customer's home phone to "thank them for their time" right after the customer leaves, the customer will not answer their home phone since they are still on the road. This strategy keeps the Sales Professional from actually talking with the customer and helps the Sales Professional get around their call reluctance.

Let's retire this insane thought of being perceived as "pushy" right now. This insane thought has prevented countless Sales Professionals from closing and has sabotaged too many Sales.

Find a place that is quiet so you can focus on this exercise for the next few minutes. Perform the following exercise to determine your degree of being perceived as "pushy".

STEP ONE:

Imagine that you are one of your customers walking up to meet you.

Picture you - being greeted by you. Watch you greet you - from your customer's eyes.

Take on the role of your customer, and *evaluate* your greeting through the eyes of your customer. Picture walking up to you; watch yourself smile, have good eye-contact, and introduce yourself. See yourself through the eyes of your customer; be warm, friendly and inviting. Watch you do one of your best greetings – now take a deep breath and relax.

Feel good - as your customer would. Feel open, and relaxed.

STEP TWO:

Now, from your customer's eyes, watch you ask some qualifying questions in a friendly manner. See you as a Sales Professional showing genuine interest in you - the customer. Start liking you - the Sales Professional.

Feel as if you are fortunate that this Sales Professional seems like a good one. You feel fortunate that you finally have a Sales Professional that you can easily talk to. Think that based on what you've seen so far, the way this Sales Professional has treated you is better than the way most other Sales Professionals have treated you.

Feel very comfortable, comfortable enough that you want to go ahead and open up to this Sales Professional and explain to them on a much deeper level what you *really want*. And share some *emotional* reasons *why* you want it.

STEP THREE:

Now that you have really opened up to you - watch as you the Sales Professional listens intently, absorbs everything you mention, and contemplates on which product to offer you. You watch you say, "Based on everything I heard, I think I have something that will work for you." Imagine that.

Watch as you the Sales Professional performs a knock-it-out-of-the-park product presentation. Watch you do tie-downs and trial closes – in a very matter-of-fact way like an emotional magnet, attracting your thoughts of thinking this product is perfect for you. Along the way imagine that you have many questions and they are all answered to your satisfaction.

You are impressed with you, the Sales Professional. You are impressed with your product knowledge and with the enthusiasm that you have about your company. You appreciate the way that you individualized the product benefits to your specific needs, as opposed to some other places that you looked and saw other Sales Professionals do generic Sales Presentations with no enthusiasm. You watched others "feature dump".

You are impressed…and almost sold.

But then, just as everything seemed like you were going to ask you, the Sales Professional, what you need to do to buy it - you have an "area of concern".

You say, " I'm not sure about this…" and something comes up that makes you unsure if it will work for you or not. You seem hesitant.

Then, you watch you, the Sales Professional, in a friendly manner, probe a little more by asking you to elaborate on what your concern is, and be more specific about what your concern is.

Think now that as a customer, you feel like the Sales Professional was on your side, and you trusted their opinion and felt comfortable that the solution they offered for your concern would work for you.

Now, though your customer's eye, watch you, the Sales Professional, ask you, "Do you have any other questions?"

As the customer, you answer, "No, I can't think of any."

Watch you, the Sales Professional, ask, "So this would work for you?"

You answer, "Yes, it would."

STEP FOUR:

Through your customer's eyes, watch you explain the buying process.

Watch you say, " If you wanted to move forward, this is what you would do." Watch you explain what the steps are and what all would happen to consummate the sale.

Here is the critical part:

Through your customer's eyes, watch you close.

See your face, listen to your tone, and listen to your words – watch you say that one little closing sentence. (Choose a closing sentence and watch you say it now in your mind.)

Did you appear "pushy"?

As the customer, did you feel all of the rapport juice drain out of your body?

Or, did being asked to buy it just seem like part of the conversation – a part that was simply connected to all of the other parts?

The distinction here is that the *imagined result* of asking for the sale does not cause someone to think that you are "not friendly" or "pushy".

Not if you included all of the ingredients – and have rapport.

In fact, if you presented urgency early and softly in your presentation as if urgency was simply a matter-of-fact, then as opposed to being perceived as pushy, in reality you would be perceived as being helpful and friendly. You would solidify that you are indeed "being friendly". It would be perceived that you are "looking out" for your newfound friend, your customer.

In a way, you would be *their hero*.

END OF EXERCISE

Answer this question: which would you rather do? Show up at the bank and:

A. Have to make a withdrawal and explain to the teller that you did not ask your customers to buy because you didn't want to change your rapport with them and seem "pushy"

B. Deposit a commission check and explain to the teller that you read this book and you started asking more people to buy, and that is how you have made so many new friends and why you are depositing so many more commission checks.

If you're really concerned about making new friends…you could make your job and adventure to find as many new friends as possible… named "Ben". Fill out the chart below.

ABUNDANCE OF NEW FRIENDS

_____ Total number of times in the last 12 months that I did not close for any reason(s), such as not wanting to reduce rapport or from leaving out ingredients (Go back and add up both previous charts.)

X _____ My average commission

= $_____ Total commissions I could have earned

= $_____ Number of Ben Franklins ($100 dollar bills) (Calculate how many Ben Franklins – for example, $1000 = 10 Bens)

That means that when I start closing like I should, there will be_____ extra Ben Franklins that are waiting to be my friend in the next 12 months.

The Myth of the Fear of Rejection

Understand another simple fact. After you ask your customer to buy, then, and only then, will the customer begin to "own it" in their mind.

Strategically, you want to know what their core beliefs are. The first time you close you want to know their deepest thoughts on buying – because either you are done selling them on your product, or you're not. When you ask them to buy, an area of concern may be presented and that is your chance to work through it.

You want this opportunity while they are still in front of you, as opposed to them solving it while sitting at your competitor's desk.

On the other hand, after you ask the customer to buy it, you may determine that the customer really is "sold", but they just won't say yes at this time. Your assessment is that they are simply *human* and humans are *procrastinators*.

This is what you want to distinguish; either they want it and won't move forward because they need help with making the "big decision", or there is something in their mind that makes them uncomfortable. Perhaps an ingredient was left out, and you need to do some more selling.

Either of the above scenarios can easily be handled with a "friendly" approach. You can let Relationship Selling work overtime for you – without any extra cost because it's a workaholic on salary. It loves what it's doing, and doing what it loves!

Most of the Sales Professionals that attend one of my Reflection Selling Workshops believe, when they walk in, that if they asked a customer to buy more than once, they definitely would appear "pushy". And when they walk out, their intellect, from within, causes them to smile when they are asked about the subject of closing – because beyond feeling comfortable closing once, they also see how closing more than once can be viewed as "friendly".

Every Sales Professional leaves my workshop with the wisdom of how to employ Relationship Selling to its fullest potential. Every Sales Professional leaves owning the belief that if the customer does not buy after being asked to, the Sales Professional will still have their newfound "friend".

Moreover, these Sales Professionals own the belief that the real reason that the customer is asked to buy is because the Sales Professional is looking out for them – that's why the Sales Professional asked them to "take it off the market" – so no one else will get it.

We leave the customer with the view that the Sales Professional will protect their newfound friend's interests, and fight off other potential buyers.

From the customer's view, you are their hero. There are other people interested in buying it too – and they are monsters!

I could elaborate here on the misuse of "urgency". Most Sales Professionals miss the opportunity to be the customer's hero at the end of a Sales Presentation when the customer does not buy. I will only touch on this subject since it is not the focus of this book, but I feel compelled to shed some light on these missed opportunities.

The majority of the time, most Sales Professionals bring up urgency at <u>the very end of the presentation</u>. In essence, they beat the customer over the head with it. They threaten the customer with something like, "It won't last long!" I have heard even worse: "It might not be here when you come back."

The urgency message is delivered from a position of force – an attack.

The message, "If you don't buy it, somebody else will," is "pushy" in my view. There is nothing "friendly" about it.

Just like mega-ships that float – hard to believe – some Sales Professionals, after not asking a closing question, simply pause towards the end of the presentation, and when the customer finally says, "Well, thank you, you've been very nice…let me think about it", that's when the Sales Professional who left out a lot of ingredients and didn't close misuses urgency – and *threatens* the customer by saying, "If you don't buy it, somebody else will!"

People really do this – and mega ships float, big planes fly – go figure.

Any *attack* will cause a *defense* — it's a universal law. There is not a seasoned Sales Professional I know of who would say they want their customers to be on the defense. Yet these same Sales Professionals don't realize that's what they are doing by threatening the customer with urgency.

Rather than tease you and leave you hanging on what would be a good way to use urgency, I will share one way with you now.

You should present urgency in the very *early* stage of your engagement, right after greeting the customer and very early on in discovering their needs and wants. It goes something like this:

The customer says, "I like the blue."

You reply, "You like the blue? That's incredible, the activity we've had on blue has been unbelievable…I wonder if it's something in the water?"

Now, if you have recently sold a lot of blues, it would be elementary to use the above statement. However, what if there hadn't been a blue sold for a long time? Well, read the words again: "I can't believe the activity we've had on blues…it must be something in the water."

Whether you've sold any or not - the statement works!

Now, you say in a matter-of-fact way that you can't believe the activity on the blues. You mention this before you really start into the product presentation. You go through your presentation, using all of the ingredients, of course, and at the end of the presentation…before you close…you simply remind the customer of what you mentioned earlier.

You say something like, "So, this works for you?"

They answer, "Yes, it would."

You reply, "I'm with you, I like blue too. This is a nice one and I can see that you would enjoy it."

Then, in a matter-of-fact and friendly way, you say, "Remember when you first came in, I mentioned that the activity level on the blue has been incredible?"

Pause and watch their reaction.

The strategy here is that, as opposed to a perceived "threat" or "Sales gimmick" of using urgency, instead, you are *reminding* your newfound friend of the urgency to purchase. The reality of losing the one-of-a-kind right product creates more urgency than any other reason.

Next, keep going and explain "how to buy". Explain the buying process.

Ask the customer, "Any questions about that?"

They answer, "No, I can't think of any."

Then close; go ahead – say that one little closing sentence.

You have successfully used urgency and closed.

Go from there.

I want you to walk away from this with the insight that real-life friends want their friends to have good things in their lives. Friends actually "push" real-life friends to buy things.

Sometimes our friends are the ones we call to help us with buying big-tickets because we trust them. Our real-life friends convince us that we deserve things when we are reluctant to buy them. Our friends can be pushy, but we allow them to be because sometimes we need to be pushed.

Our friends close us.

Rent this view – go ahead – make a friend with your customer, listen and recognize your newfound friend's emotional needs, present urgency early, sell to satisfy those needs, justify the purchase with the facts and logic, and be "friendly" and ask them to buy.

You and your customer deserve it.

Chapter Highlights

Relationship Selling can easily be misunderstood, and that could lead to limited sales.

In the worst cases, as opposed to helping make the sale, Relationship Selling sabotages the sale.

Relationship Selling is the most powerful tool available when used properly at closing.

Do you see yourself as "pushy"? If not, then wouldn't it be okay if you -- closed you?

SIX

BE AWARE

In this chapter we will identify the last couple of reasons why you might not be closing. I could have written this book in an instruction-style format and included computer printouts, with facts and figures showing which reason for not closing happens most often, which is second, third, etc. But as I mentioned earlier, Sales is personal, and I intended for you to explore *your* Sales Presentations and become aware of why *you* don't close like *you* should.

You have probably heard by now that people are creatures of habit. If you disagree with that, that's O.K., but the next time you get out of the shower, be aware of how you dry yourself off. You will notice that you are drying yourself off just like you did the last 500 times.

You developed a pattern – a habit – and it worked, so why focus on trying to change it? Drying yourself fell into an insignificant part of your life and drying off can be done at an unconscious level.

It's called unconscious competence.

And in the same way that drying yourself off is an insignificant act in your life that you do in your daily routine, other, more complicated actions have developed into habits that we do at a lower level of conscious awareness. Although some actions we do are more complicated, as a result of doing them repeatedly, we perform these more complicated acts at a level of unconscious competence as well.

Driving a car is a perfect example.

You think I'm kidding? Remember the *first* time you drove a car? Maybe it was in driver's education in high school. Maybe a friend or family member let you drive for the very first time. During the very first time you were navigating the car by yourself, you were very conscious, alert, and aware of everything about navigating the car. Then, over time, your level of awareness lowered to a level of near auto-pilot. Some people run stop signs, run red lights, change lanes without looking first and do other dumb things while driving a car – because they are operating at a level of unconscious competence.

Some people text while driving. It's scary, but true.

In the same context, many Sales Professionals that have performed the same *planned presentation* many times have developed habits. Some are good habits; some are not so good. Some Sales Professionals, through conscious repetition, have developed a good habit of saying something specific in every Sales Presentation they make. It could be something about their company, their quality, or their service. They want to make sure they say it every time. The Sales Professional says it so many times that it becomes habit – unconscious competence.

I need not expand on the thought that some Sales Professionals leave out some ingredients and shorten their presentations. By doing so in repetition, they develop bad habits and their presentation defaults to being performed at a level of unconscious competence – and their success is limited, to say the least.

You want to make closing a *good habit* for you. Become aware that you want to include all of the ingredients and perform a complete presentation, so that all fear is removed at closing.

Start thinking that your intention at the end of your presentation is to close. Make sure that at a *conscious* level you do.

Repeat this often enough so it becomes anchored in your mind.

Just think, if it all worked out, you would be *closing* at a level of *unconscious competence!* It will become a good habit.

This chapter is focused on identifying another couple of reasons why you are not closing as often as you would like to – and how to conquer them.

Awareness is a word that you want to adopt in your life; not just in Sales, but in all aspects of your life. *Awareness* gives you *power* in any area of your life that you are operating on a near-unconscious or unconscious level.

Take a relationship with a significant other for example. If you operate in that relationship in "the same ol' routine" manner, and if you have developed habits that are not rewarding you with an extraordinary relationship, *awareness* will give you the power to make that relationship better.

Of course, *desire* is at the core of influencing your actions. If you have no desire, you can be aware of your actions…your not-so-good habits… but without desire, you will take no positive action and remain in the same undesirable routine.

Making repeated Sales Presentations, whether good or bad, can easily become habitual and routine in nature. The action only needs to be repeated enough for it to become a habit. The mind accepts all repetitive actions and responds accordingly.

At the core of wanting to make an "A Game" presentation you will find *desire*. By getting in touch with your inner desire, you will be aware of your actions in your presentation. Your awareness will allow you to be focused at the end of your presentation and you will feel comfortable to close. In this scenario, you will be fully relaxed and "present" with the customer in front of you. It is in this environment that your chances of closing are at an optimum level.

You must be *present* to close.

PRESENT TO CLOSE

If a football team was ahead 45 to 0 at half time, but did not come out of the locker room to finish playing the game, then even though they were way ahead in points, they would not win. They must be present at the end of the game to win. It's the rules.

So goes the Sales Game.

In other words, let's say that you did a knock-it-out-of-the-park greeting; you really made the customer feel comfortable – you made a friend. And you did a great presentation, asked all of the great questions and had all of the great answers. It was your "A Game" presentation. But if you are not present at closing, you won't make the sale. It's the rules of the game.

"Be present at closing" sounds pretty simple, doesn't it? It's simple, but not easy.

Let's make a distinction here. Simply identifying and acknowledging a simple solution to a problem does not *solve* the problem. Accepting a simple action like changing our light bulbs to energy-smart, compact, fluorescent light bulbs doesn't lower our country's energy consumption. Taking action – *changing* the light bulbs – will lower our country's energy consumption.

The "must be present to close" solution is easy to understand, but a little challenging to do. There are many reasons that would cause a Sales Professional to not be totally present when performing their presentation.

For starters, as you know, a Sales Presentation that has been performed many times can be done without much conscious thought – done with unconscious competence.

Even before a Sales Professional greets a customer and starts a presentation, the Sales Professional may not be totally present. They may be thinking when they start working that they probably won't be making presentations to quality customers that day because it's "slow right now" – and as they are daydreaming about how slow it is, one walks in.

Being *present* and *aware* of what you do is the first step.

At the core of what you do in your presentation must be the *desire* to make the Sale. Be aware that there will be many circumstances which will attempt to steal your desire. Sales People's gossip, negative news, and slow Sales "forecasts" are things that attempt to steal your desire to sell.

Be aware of what you think about. Be aware of outside influences, and show up to work with no preconceived expectations, other than that you will greet every customer expecting to sell them.

If it's so easy, why don't Sales Professionals just show up, stay present and sell?

Because sometimes, "It" stops them. "It" blocks them from selling.

BE AWARE OF "IT"

I showed up once at a car dealership wanting to buy two cars. It was a reality that I hated to face, but I had procrastinated in replacing cars. I needed one and my son needed one. We were running on old, high-mileage cars, and they were breaking down. It was becoming a nuisance.

One day, I got a call from the mechanic at the auto repair shop. After he told me how much the repair was going to be for one of the cars, I blew a fuse. I announced that I had enough of this, and that I was going to buy two new cars and be done with it!

At the first dealership, I was met by a young man who seemed friendly. He asked the typical qualifying question, "What are you looking for?"

I answered, "Actually, I need two cars."

Immediately upon hearing my response of needing two cars, I saw "It" hit him, and "It" hit him hard! His head jerked back and he was consumed with disbelief. "It" must have told him, "No way!" "It" must have told him, "No way are you going to sell this guy two cars – you're wasting your time." I can further speculate that "It" called me a flake inside this Salesman's head.

For all intents and purposes, I am referring to "It" as that little voice inside your head. Some people label "It" as simply our self-talk, that internal dialogue that only you hear inside your head. It tells you what to do. Sometimes you do what it tells you to do; sometimes you argue with it and don't.

It influences your thoughts about most everything that you do on a conscious level – some say on an unconscious level. Some say it can also produce dreams and cause you to make decisions based on your interpretation of those dreams.

"It" is powerful.

Back to the above-mentioned Car Salesman. It told him there was no such thing as making two Sales to one customer. In reality, I showed up to his dealership in the market for two cars. The end result was that I didn't buy even one car from this Salesman. It told him to hurry up and drop me. He obeyed It's command.

I went on to look at more cars for a few minutes and then walked to the dealership next door. There was a stretch of several car dealerships that were all next door to each other, so I visited several dealers that day.

After a couple of dealerships, I learned a new phrase that can get rid of almost any Car Salesman.

Just tell them you need two cars.

Notice I said "need" two cars, not that I "wanted" them – I "needed" them. If anyone had ever been present to that word "needed", they might have explored further what that "need" was. But "It" slapped the few Salesmen I saw that day into disbelief. Each of these Salesmen allowed "It" to influence their thoughts and dictate their actions.

It caused each one of them to lose two Sales.

After I became aware of the control "It" had in this scenario, I adjusted my shopping for two cars to buying only one car at a time from two different dealerships. I ended up buying two cars from two dealerships – even though in reality, I was ready, willing and able to buy both at one dealership.

No Salesmen was really aware of how "It" was influencing them and no Salesman I met could control "It".

"It" convinced them that they were *not* going to sell two cars to me – so they didn't.

When we examine it a little closer, we could say that if any of the above Salesmen were to clear their minds, be in a frame of mind of "nothing" as they qualified me, and if they were just "present" to me, they would have been able to subdue "It". The Sales Professionals would not have allowed "It" to influence their thoughts and dictate their actions.

The key to all of this is being *aware* of "It" in the first place.

Without going too far into la-la land, but to really make this clear, imagine this:

What if you told a monk, right after his meditation, that you needed three cars?

His response, with no emotion, might be, "What kind?"

You would probably continue the conversation with the monk, and in a matter-of-fact, logical, and make-sense manner you would work together and end up with a clear picture of the three cars you wanted. If the monk were working as a Sales Professional, odds are high that you would have bought three cars from him that day.

What do a monk and a Car Salesman have in common?

They are both *human;* they each have a body and a brain.

Most likely, the monk would be far more *aware* of how his brain works than the Car Salesman. The monk can identify "It". When "It" wants to influence the monk's thoughts, the monk is aware of it.

"It" is powerless over the monk.

In all fairness, the Car Salesman probably has more product knowledge than the monk.

The beauty here is that both individuals can acquire the other's knowledge. The focus of this book is not that Sales Professionals should be more like monks – although that wouldn't be a bad thing. You see, monks would enter a Sales Presentation and *assume nothing.*

A monk would be *present* to every customer, and interact with them as just another fellow human being. The monk would listen intently to the customer. Most likely, the monk would include all of the ingredients. He would make a complete presentation as opposed to half-baking one. And after confirming that the customer had found the right product and had no further questions, the monk would have no "fear of rejection".

To the monk, the closing is only another sentence. It's simply the one that comes at the end of the presentation. The monk is aware that like all things, the close is not separate, but *connected* to the *whole* presentation. He is enlightened with the insight that the closing sentence is just like the other sentences – they are all made up of the same matter – words. Each word connects to the other.

The awareness and insight which monks possess is not the focus here—you not closing is. This book was to enlighten you as to why you may not be closing like you should.

Being aware of your internal talk, of how "It" might influence your thoughts and dictate your actions, is one of those reasons. Leaving out ingredients and being afraid of losing your newfound friend are some others.

Remember, ease, clarity, and humor work.

It is Landmark Education that I credit for providing me awareness of "It". I invite you to give Landmark Education the opportunity to share this and other insights with you. It is a sad fact that our formal education system provides little-to-no education of how our minds really work and what it's like to operate as human beings. We are rarely provided insight on what reality is – and how we assign our interpretation to reality – and then make our views real.

The following is a simple example of how much in reality you might be living vs. how much you might be living in your *interpretation* of reality:

You make a presentation to a customer and they don't buy. Of course you closed; you read this book, and you now close after every complete presentation.

But since they didn't buy, and you know that they are qualified to buy and are good prospects, you now follow up with your customer and call them.

You leave them a voice mail. But they don't call you back. You ask yourself, "Why don't they call me back?"

In reality, why didn't they call you back? You might think of one of the following reasons:

> Maybe they bought somewhere else.
>
> Maybe they are not going to buy anything.
>
> Maybe they are no longer your friend because you asked them to buy at the end of the presentation...just kidding.
>
> Maybe they are too busy and will get back to you later.

Maybe they will be a "be-back" next month and will be a sale next month... just being funny again.

In reality, why didn't they call you back?

What is perfectly "normal" to do here is pick a reason, whichever reason that you like the best, and assign that reason to why they didn't call you back.

Reality is that you worked a customer, followed up with them, and they *haven't called you back.* That's *reality* - that's all there is - *there is nothing else.*

You simply called someone and *they did not call you back...yet.*

But "It" plays you. "It" provides you with a list of reasons to choose from. "It" influences you to choose a reason – and believe that it's real. A common thought process is to pick one of the reasons above - then assign that reason to reality. You actually make the reason you picked *real.*

How far does this go? How about: you *know* they probably bought from the competition; after all, you had all that rapport going and they really liked you. And they liked your product too. But the Salesperson at your competitor caught them and slammed your product – then offered them a better deal.

You *know* it.

Want to take it further? You're the one making all this up anyway.

How about you told your boss recently that your competitor is giving away the farm to make Sales – and now you just lost another one, because you called your customer that you had great rapport with…and they won't call you back!

See how this works?

And this was using a simple phone call as an example. How do you think "It" can influence your thoughts and dictate your actions with other things, not just in Sales, but in all of the other areas in your life?

We could take the above example and explore further how just the interpretation of no return phone call could cause more damage to an individual who is not aware.

Be aware of "It". As long as you are unaware, it will keep you living in dissatisfaction. When you are *aware*, "It" has little-to-no power over you. Your *intellect* takes command. Your intellect does you right… every time.

Even when your intellect has influenced your good judgment and causes you to take the right action or to make the right choice, "It" will constantly nag at you and tell you that you were wrong.

Stay present. Be aware of "It". You'll not only close more deals, but you'll find more joy in the other areas of your life as well.

IN CLOSING

There are many reasons why you might not be closing. This book has made you aware of several things to look out for. Hopefully, by now, you have not only identified which reason(s) have prevented you from closing, but you have started on thoughts about what actions to take to make closing a good habit. You now see closing as something that is simply connected to the end of your presentation. The myth of the fear of rejection has been busted.

There was no order of importance in the way this book was written. I did not start with the biggest or smallest reason why Sales Professionals don't close. All of the reasons in this book are important, and you definitely want to be aware of them all. This book was all about *you* and *your closing*.

Let's review some of the reasons why you might not be closing like you should.

In the first chapter, we identified that many Sales Professionals do not perform a complete presentation; they leave out some of the ingredients. Therefore, they do not feel comfortable closing – simple and easy to see.

In Chapter Two, we became aware of the fact that some Sales Professionals perform a complete presentation, and at the end of the presentation, the Sales Professional is definitely in a logical, make-sense position to close. But they don't close – because they do not want to change the rapport they have with their customer, their newfound friend.

We recognized the misunderstanding of Relationship Selling. We concluded that not closing because the customer may not consider you friendly was simply not true. Wouldn't your *friend* tell you to buy something? Wouldn't your friend inform you of urgency as a matter-of-fact? In other words, your real-life friend would say, "You better get one, because they are almost out," or "They are selling them pretty fast." Your *friend* closes you. This insight will overcome the limits and even sabotages of Relationship Selling and will allow you to generate more sales.

The last chapter explained that you need to be aware of "It". Label "It" what you want, but "It" is simply your self-talk, which has enough power to influence your thoughts and dictate your actions. "It" only has power when you are unaware of it doing so. By identifying it, "It" loses its power and no longer drives you. Your intellect takes the keys and steers you to success.

Close more – sell more. You may as well have some fun while you're at it.

Share this.

Chapter Highlights

Be conscious of your thoughts; they develop into your actions, and your actions over time become your habits.

Good or bad -- either way, your habits define your results in life.

You must be "present" to close. If you are not present at the end of the game, you forfeit.

Choose to make closing an unconscious, conscious habit.

ABOUT THE AUTHOR

Mike Jackson is the founder of Progressive Insights, Inc., a Sales Training and Personal Development organization. His delivery of critical performance topics via humor, ease, and clarity results in measurable success.

Mike authored the Reflection Selling program, a comprehensive Sales Training and Personal Development program. Since 1996, Mike has trained countless Sales Professionals across North America, and is a leading expert in Selling Strategies and Personal Development for Sales Professionals, Sales Managers and Business Owners.

Mike is the author of <u>Cherry Picking – If the Cherries Aren't Low Enough…Get a Ladder!</u>, available on <u>Amazon.com</u> or in your favorite bookstore. He is also available for one- and two-day workshops, and as a keynote speaker on multiple subjects. For more information on these and other services, please visit <u>ReflectionSelling.com</u>.

Mike enjoys world travel.